DRAGONFLIES

DRAGONFLIES

by Cynthia Overbeck

Photographs by Yuko Sato

A Lerner Natural Science Book

Lerner Publications Company ▪ Minneapolis

Sylvia A. Johnson, Series Editor

Translation of original text by Kay Kushino

Photographs on pages 6, 17, 23, 27, and 44 by Klaus Paysan

The publisher wishes to thank Jerry W. Heaps,
Department of Entomology, University of Minnesota,
for his assistance in the preparation of this book.

The glossary on page 46 gives definitions and pronunciations of
words shown in **bold type** in the text.

LIBRARY OF CONGRESS CATALOGING IN PUBLICATION DATA

Overbeck, Cynthia
  Dragonflies.

    (A Lerner natural science book)
    Adaptation of: Akatombo no isshō/by Yūkō Satō.
    Includes index.
    Summary: Introduces dragonflies and damselflies,
  closely related winged insects which undergo a three-
  stage process of development called incomplete metamorphosis.
      1. Dragonflies—Juvenile literature. 2. Damselflies—
  Juvenile literature. [1. Dragonflies. 2. Damselflies.
  3. Insects] I. Satō, Yūko, 1928-   ill. II. Satō, Yūko,
  1928-   . Akatombo no isshō. III. Title. IV. Series.
  QL520.087   595.7'33   82-7221
  ISBN 0-8225-1477-X (lib. bdg.)   AACR2

This edition first published 1982 by Lerner Publications Company.
Text copyright © 1982 by Lerner Publications Company.
Photographs copyright © 1971 by Yuko Sato. Adapted from LIFE
OF THE RED DRAGONFLY copyright © 1971 by Yuko Sato.
English language rights arranged by Kurita-Bando Literary Agency
for Akane Shobo Publishers, Tokyo, Japan.

International Standard Book Number: 0-8225-1477-X
Library of Congress Catalog Card Number: 82-7221

    2   3   4   5   6   7   8   9   10   90   89   88   87   86   85   84   83

If you sit quietly by a pond or stream on a warm summer day, you may see some large flying insects darting through the air or hovering like tiny helicopters over the water. Their long bodies are slim as needles and often brightly colored. Their transparent wings flash in the sun and make a loud buzzing sound as they move rapidly up and down.

These beautiful insects are called dragonflies. This common name was given to them because they look something like small winged dragons. Scientists classify dragonflies as members of the order Odonata, along with their close relatives the damselflies. In the following pages, you will learn about the lives and habits of this fascinating group of insects.

c. LB

This modern dragonfly is much smaller than the giant dragonflies of prehistoric times.

Dragonflies have been around for a very long time. They were among the earliest flying insects to evolve on earth, first appearing more than 300 million years ago. These early dragonflies were quite large; some of them had wingspans of two feet (70 centimeters) or more. By 180 million years ago, the prehistoric giants had developed into insects with the same basic size and body structure as the dragonflies we see today. Modern dragonflies have an average wingspan of three to four inches (6.5-10 centimeters), although some measure as much as six inches (15 centimeters) across their wings.

Damselflies are generally smaller than dragonflies. There are also minor differences in body structure and habits between the two groups of Odonata insects. But in their basic ways of living, the 5,000 species, or kinds, of dragonflies and damselflies are very much alike. The insects are found all over the world, wherever there are freshwater ponds, streams, or lakes. In the early stages of their lives, dragonflies and damselflies live entirely in the water. As adults, they may wander miles away from the pond or stream to search for food in forests and fields. The insects usually return to water to mate and lay their eggs.

Dragonflies and damselflies are most familiar to us in their winged adult forms. But the insects look very different in the early stages of their lives. There are three separate stages in the development of dragonflies and damselflies, and in each stage, the insects go through a change in form. This process of development is called **incomplete metamorphosis**. Insects such as butterflies and moths go through a four-stage development known as **complete metamorphosis**.

Left: A cluster of dragon-fly eggs, magnified many times. *Opposite*: A dragon-fly nymph hatches. The long body and the head with its black eyes have emerged from the egg. The legs are still folded up inside.

Dragonflies and damselflies begin their lives as tiny eggs. This is the first stage in the process that will produce adult insects. Female dragonflies and damselflies lay their eggs in ponds, streams, and other bodies of water. Some are deposited in the water, while others are attached to the stem of a water plant. The eggs may be laid one by one or in a cluster made up of as many as 800 eggs.

Once laid, the eggs either cling to underwater plants or sink to the bottom of the pond. They are anchored by tiny threads or by a sticky substance that covers them.

After going through a period of development in the water, a dragonfly or damselfly egg hatches. The creature that comes out of the egg is called a **nymph**. It is the second stage of incomplete metamorphosis. The nymphal stage lasts from several months to more than three years, depending on the species of dragonfly or damselfly. It is the longest stage in the insects' development.

8

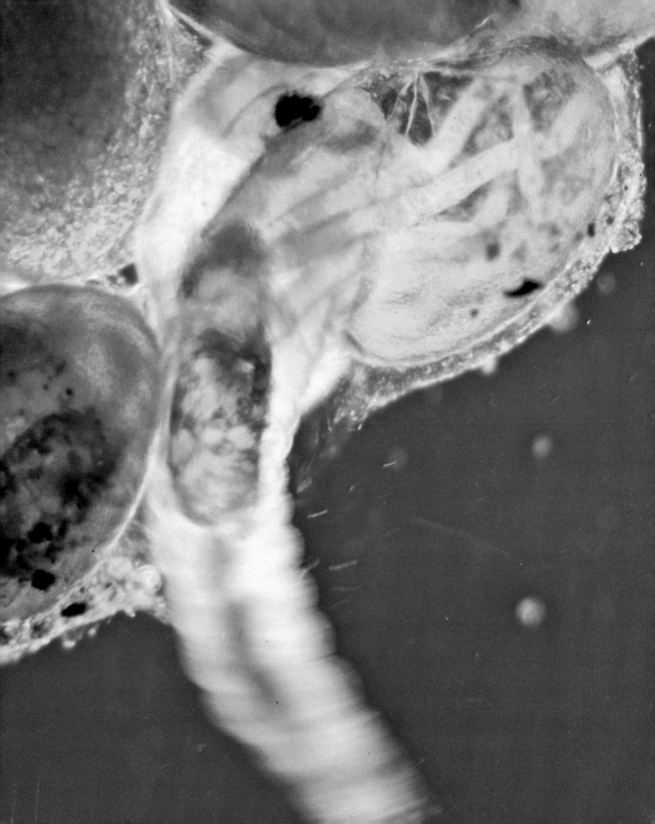

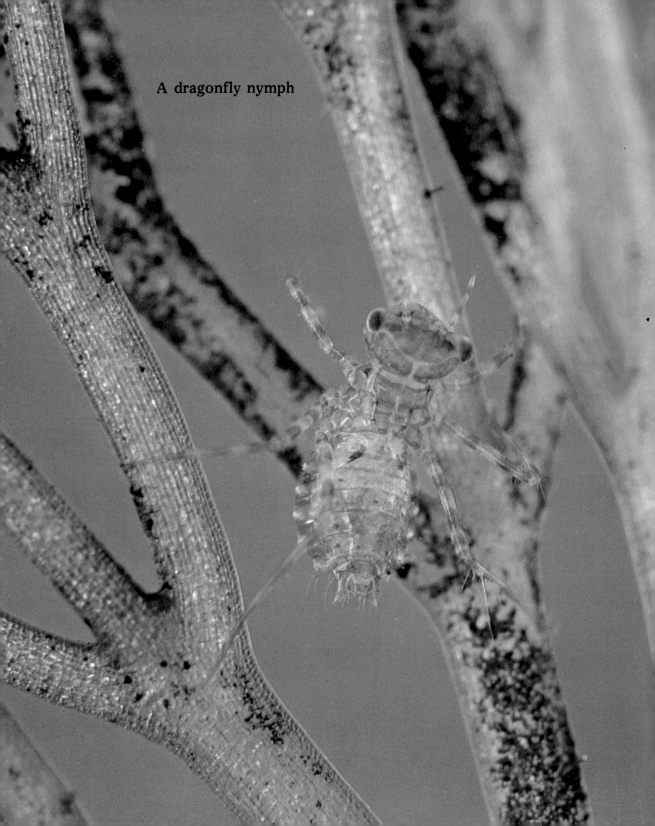

A dragonfly nymph

When a nymph first hatches, it is very tiny—less than 1/16 inch (about 1.2 millimeters) in length. But it will not stay this small for long. By the end of its development, a dragonfly or damselfly nymph may be more than 1 inch (25 millimeters) long, about 20 times its original size.

The nymph's body grows much larger, but its skin does not grow along with it. Unlike human skin, a nymph's skin does not stretch. In order to continue its development, the nymph must shed its old skin from time to time and grow a new one. This process is called **molting**.

During molting, the old skin splits open and the nymph wiggles out. Its body is covered by a new, larger skin that has formed under the old skin. The new skin is soft at first, but it soon hardens to form a protective covering for the nymph's body. An Odonata nymph usually molts 10 to 15 times during the nymphal stage.

When it is not molting, a nymph spends its time eating. For the first few days after it hatches, it is nourished by yolk material from the egg that is stored in its body. Once this food is used up, the nymph begins the life of a **predator**, or hunter.

The young nymph has a huge appetite. Fortunately, the pond or stream is full of creatures that it can hunt and eat. Its favorite prey are other immature insects, especially mosquitoes. As the nymph grows, it adds larger creatures like tadpoles and shellfish to its diet. Some nymphs will even attack young fish as big as themselves.

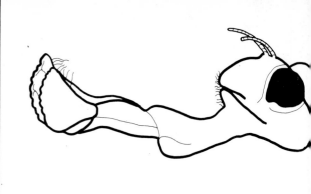

Above left: A dragonfly nymph captures a mosquito with its extended labium. *Above right*: This drawing shows the parts of the labium. *Opposite*: This nymph's labium is folded under its head like a mask.

Nymphs generally hunt by lying in wait for their prey rather than by chasing it. Some hide in the mud on the pond bottom. Others crawl up the stems of underwater plants and sit there quietly. When the prey moves within range, the nymph creeps a little closer. Then, with lightning speed, it whips out a special lower lip to catch the animal. This lip, or **labium**, is unique in the insect world. It is made up of two flat plates hinged together and attached to the lower part of the nymph's head. When not in use, the lip is folded beneath the head and looks like a long, triangular mask.

When the nymph spots a meal, the labium suddenly unhinges and shoots forward. Fully opened, it may measure half the length of the nymph's body. The labium has pincer-like "graspers" at the end, equipped with bristles. These graspers grab the prey and pull it back into the nymph's mouth. Sharp **mandibles**, or jaws, then chew up the prey.

A dragonfly nymph in the final stage of its development

Except for its unusual lip, the nymph has the same basic body parts that all insects have. The body is divided into three main sections: the head, thorax, and abdomen. These parts will remain generally the same in the adult dragonfly or damselfly as they are in the nymph. But the forms of some of its organs will change as the insect develops.

On the nymph's head are its mouthparts and most of its sense organs. The nymph has two short, slender **antennae**, organs that are sensitive to touch. The antennae are larger in the nymphal stage than they will be in the adult stage. Of great importance to the insect in both stages are its eyes. The two eyes are large and bulging, and they provide excellent vision. The eyes will reach their fullest stage of development in the adult.

Attached to the nymph's **thorax**, the middle part of its body, are three pairs of slender legs. As an adult, the dragonfly or damselfly will not use its legs for walking. But the nymph is a fairly strong walker and often depends on its legs to get around underwater. The thorax is also the part of the body where the **wing pads** develop. These structures begin to appear around the time of the third molt. They contain the veins and tissues that will become wings in the adult insect.

The abdomen of the nymph is shorter and wider than it will be in the adult. It is divided in segments or sections. In the abdomen are the insect's digestive system and its developing reproductive system. The abdomen also includes the organs used for breathing.

In the nymphal stage, as in later adulthood, there are some differences between the bodies of dragonflies and those of damselflies. The dragonfly nymph has a short, thick body and very small antennae. The damselfly nymph has a longer, more slender body, a smaller head, and longer antennae. The two kinds of nymphs also differ in the arrangement of their breathing organs. Both breathe through **gills,** in much the same way that fish do. The gills pull in fresh water and, with it, dissolved oxygen. The oxygen is absorbed and used in the body, and the water is expelled.

In the dragonfly nymph, the gills are located inside the rear of the abdomen. Waste water is expelled in a jet from an opening at the end of the abdomen. This jet of water helps the dragonfly nymph to swim rapidly. When threatened, the nymph moves in quick jerks, propelled by spurts of water.

The damselfly's gills form a fan-like tail attached to the end of the abdomen. They also absorb oxygen and expel waste water. But the damselfly nymph does not depend on jets of water to help it swim. Instead, it swims by wiggling its gills in the same way that a fish wiggles its tail.

Both kinds of nymphs often need to move quickly in order to escape the frogs, water beetles, and other animals that prey on them. Nymphs also avoid predators simply by sitting still. The colors and markings on their bodies blend in with their surroundings, making them hard to see.

If a nymph is not attacked by predators, it will continue to eat and grow. Finally the time will come for the nymph to move into the last stage of its development and become

This picture clearly shows the fanlike gills of a damselfly nymph.

an adult dragonfly or damselfly. During the nymphal stage, its body has been getting ready for this great change. Now it is time for the nymph to leave the water and begin its life as a winged adult.

During the dark of the night, the nymph crawls out of the water for the first time in its life. Depending on the species, it finds a perch on a floating leaf or on a rock or plant stem on the shore. There it clings in the darkness, waiting for the tremendous change to happen.

Several hours pass. At last the outer skin dries out and splits open along the back. The adult's moist body begins to squeeze out. It is a great struggle. The head emerges (left), then the thorax, and finally the long abdomen. At first the dragonfly is hanging upside down (center). Then it rights itself and clings, exhausted, to its old skin (right).

After it first emerges, the dragonfly's body seems fat and bloated, and its wings look like small, crumpled stumps (left). But in the next few hours, blood is pumped from the body into the veins, and the wings stiffen, dry, and expand (right). By the time the morning sun appears, the dragonfly's metamorphosis is complete.

Opposite: **A dragonfly dries its newly opened wings in the sun.** *Above left*: **The damselfly has a very slender body.** *Above right*: **The body of a dragonfly has a slightly flattened look.**

It is hard to believe that this elegant creature with its gauzy wings developed from the clumsy-looking nymph that spent its life on the bottom of the pond. In their adult forms, both dragonflies and damselflies have long abdomens that are often brightly colored in reds, blues, and greens. The abdomen of a damselfly is thin and rounded, sometimes almost needle-like in appearance. A dragonfly's abdomen is usually slightly flattened.

Along each side of the adult Odonata's abdomen is a row of breathing holes, or **spiracles**, that are connected to a system of tubes inside the body. This respiratory system, which has replaced the nymph's gills, allows the adult insect to take in oxygen from the air.

21

The thorax of an adult dragonfly or damselfly seems large in contrast to the slender abdomen. It contains powerful muscles needed to work the all-important wings. The two pair of wings are attached to the back part of the thorax and are of about equal length. (In dragonflies, the back pair is wider at the base than the front pair.)

The wings are large in proportion to the insects' bodies. They are made of layers of very thin, transparent membrane supported by a framework of tiny veins. The veins form a variety of complicated patterns that differ from species to species. These patterns are often useful to scientists in

A damselfly's large thorax contains powerful muscles that move the wings.

In many species of dragonflies, the adult male (right) is more brightly colored than the female (left).

identifying the various kinds of dragonflies and damselflies.

In some species, the wings have colorful markings—spots or bars of blue, yellow, black, or other colors. These beautiful colors are produced in several different ways. Some of them are caused by pigments, chemicals in the outer layers of the wings. Other colors are produced by light striking the surface of the wings in special ways. (The colors on the insects' bodies are produced by these same two methods.)

Some dragonflies and damselflies have wings that look **iridescent**; that is, they shine with lovely rainbow-like colors. This iridescence is caused by sunlight striking a thin liquid suspended between the layers of the wings. When the insects die, the liquid dries up and the glowing color disappears.

This dragonfly has wings of vivid yellow.

The Odonata are famous not only for the beauty of their wings but also for the power and grace of their flight. The two pair of wings work efficiently together to help a dragonfly or damselfly maneuver skillfully in the air.

In many four-winged insects, the front and hind wings on each side are locked together and move as one. But in damselflies and dragonflies, each pair of wings moves independently during flight. When the front pair lifts upward, the rear pair beats downward. Both pairs get additional lift by twisting a little with every beat. This gives a sort of oar-like dip and roll to each wing movement.

As this dragonfly alights on a twig, high-speed photography captures the separate movements of its two pairs of wings.

Generally, dragonflies are better fliers than damselflies. Unless they are alarmed, damselflies usually have a slow, fluttering style of flying. But dragonflies are strong and fast. They can dart and dodge with great speed and agility.

Different species of dragonflies have different patterns of flight. Some fly high above the treetops, while others skim low over ponds and streams. Some patrol back and forth over a certain section of a pond, along a regular route.

Some types of dragonflies are even long-distance fliers. From time to time, usually in the autumn, thousands of dragonflies gather and fly together, sometimes hundreds of miles, to a new territory. No one knows exactly why these migrations occur.

But normally, dragonflies and damselflies do not stray many miles from their original homes. In the forests and fields near their ponds, they spend their adult lives in a continual hunt for food. Usually they hunt during the day, for they are sun-loving insects. Their main sources of food are other flying insects that they must catch on the wing. To be successful hunters, they must fly fast enough and well enough to capture insects such as mosquitoes, flies, gnats, and bees that are themselves master fliers. They must be able to change directions abruptly and dart quickly from side to side, or backward or forward, to grab their prey.

Strong wings, keen vision, sharp jaws, and powerful legs
all contribute to making the dragonfly one of the most
successful hunters in the air.

Left: A damselfly's compound eyes bulge out on the sides of its head. *Opposite*: The dragonfly's huge eyes meet on top of its head.

In addition to flying skills, dragonflies and damselflies need good vision to be successful hunters. In order to spot prey, they must be able to see around, above, and below them. They must also be able to spot objects at a distance.

The huge eyes of dragonflies and damselflies are specially made for hunting in the air. They are the most obvious features on the insects' heads. A dragonfly's eyes almost meet on top of the head. The eyes of a damselfly are rounder and bulge out on both sides of the insect's head. These complicated visual organs are called **compound eyes**.

Compound eyes are made up of many individual parts called **facets**. In damselflies and dragonflies, each eye may have 25,000 or more facets. Each facet is a tiny, six-sided lens. The lenses are arranged on a curve so that each focuses in a slightly different direction.

28

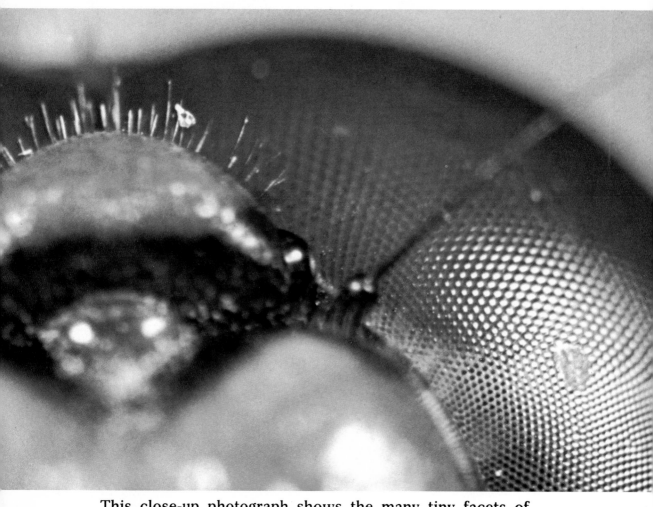

This close-up photograph shows the many tiny facets of a dragonfly's compound eye.

Alone, each lens records only one small section of the scene before it. But when the sections recorded by all the lenses come together in the insect's brain, they combine to form a complete image. The sections fit together almost like the pieces of a mosaic or a jigsaw puzzle.

Because of the curved shape of their eyes, dragonflies and damselflies can see in several directions at one time. Their heads also turn very freely, and this helps to widen their range of vision even more.

The insects' sharp eyes can also see objects at a distance. Studies have shown that they can spot objects up to 40 feet (11.7 meters) away—a great distance for an insect.

In addition to compound eyes, damselflies and dragonflies have three simple, light-sensitive eyes called **ocelli** on top of their heads. Many insects have this same combination of eyes, but no other group has the keenness and range of vision of the Odonata.

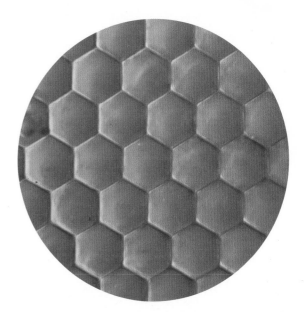

A highly magnified picture showing the individual facets of the eye

The eyes of some dragonflies are brightly colored.

Damselflies (left) and dragonflies (opposite) have spiny legs with sharp hooks on the ends.

With the aid of their sharp vision and powerful wings, dragonflies and damselflies can easily hunt down their quick-moving prey. Once they catch up with a potential meal, they have a unique way of capturing it. They seize it with their long, thin legs.

The six legs of an Odonata insect are located near the front of its thorax. They are fringed with rows of sharp little spines. At the end of each leg are tiny hooked claws. As a dragonfly or damselfly zooms through the air, it holds the first two pairs of legs crooked together to form a kind of basket (shown in the picture on the opposite page). When it spots a mosquito or other prey, it scoops it up in this basket. The spines on the legs grip the insect so that it can't escape.

32

This dragonfly is using its forelegs to stuff an insect into its mouth.

When a dragonfly has captured an insect, it stuffs it into its mouth immediately and chews it up with strong, sharp mandibles. Damselflies usually land and perch on a plant stem while they eat.

35

A dragonfly clings to its perch on a twig.

Although the legs of dragonflies and damselflies are useful for capturing prey, they are too weak for walking. Since the insects spend most of their time in the air, walking is not necessary. But both kinds of Odonata need to alight on a twig or stalk once in a while to rest and, in the case of the damselfly, to eat. When they want to perch, they use the claws at the ends of their legs to cling securely to the spot.

Once a dragonfly or damselfly chooses a particular spot on a plant or rock, it will return to it almost every time it wants to rest. Sometimes groups of these insects gather on the stalks of certain plants and rest together.

When at rest, dragonflies cannot fold their wings flat against their bodies in the way that insects such as beetles or bugs can. Instead, they hold their wings straight out, parallel to the ground. Damselflies, on the other hand, usually bring their wings together over their bodies to form a kind of steeple.

Left: A dragonfly becomes the prey of a frog. *Right*: A damselfly is trapped on a sticky insect-eating plant.

Whether they are perched on a twig or flying through the air, dragonflies and damselflies are never completely safe from danger. These fierce hunters are themselves hunted by many other animals. Birds, frogs, snakes, spiders and insects consider them a tasty meal.

Some dragonflies and damselflies become the prey of spiders when they fly into delicate webs spun across open spaces and flyways. Others are captured on the sticky surfaces of meat-eating plants, perhaps after they have chased a smaller insect into the plant's clutches. Still others are snapped up by birds in the air or by quick-tongued frogs lying in wait near ponds and streams.

This dragonfly has been captured by a spider.

The dragonflies and damselflies that survive such a fate go on to fulfill the most important role of their adult lives: mating and producing offspring. During this important period of their lives, the insects behave in very special ways.

Most of the mating activities of dragonflies and damselflies take place in the air. First, the male stakes out his mating territory above a section of his home pond or stream. He patrols the area, attacking and driving away any other males that wander into it. But when a female of his own species comes near, he approaches her on more friendly terms. First he displays his beautiful colors and patterns. Then he grasps the female behind the head, using a special pair of claspers called **cerci**, which are located at the end of his abdomen.

In order for the actual mating to take place, the female must twist her body around so that the tip of her abdomen touches the front part of the male's abdomen. On this area of the male's body is a special receptacle containing male sex cells, or sperm. In mating, the sperm are transferred from the male's body to the female's body. When the sperm unite with, or fertilize, the egg cells in the female's body, new life begins to develop.

As soon as mating has been completed, the female dragonfly or damselfly is ready to lay her eggs. Females of some species fly off alone to do the job. Others are accompanied by the males.

The large picture shows a male dragonfly grasping a female behind the head before mating. In the smaller picture, the two insects are mating on a plant stalk.

This male dragonfly is clasping his mate while she lays her eggs in the water.

Sometimes the male simply hovers above the female as she lays her eggs. But in some species, the male actually continues to clasp the female behind the head as she makes her rounds. He may be acting as a kind of guard or decoy to keep birds or other enemies away from his mate.

Female dragonflies and damselflies have several different ways of laying their eggs. Some fly low over the surface of a pond or stream. They touch down now and then to dip the ends of their abdomens in the water. At the end of a female's abdomen is a tiny egg-laying tube called an **ovipositor** (shown in the picture on the right). With each dip, a few eggs are ejected from the ovipositor into the water, where they sink to the bottom. One kind of damselfly actually dives underwater to lay her eggs, remaining submerged for up to half an hour.

Some females perch on water plants and use their ovipositors to insert their eggs into the stems. Others lay their eggs in wet wood. Usually the eggs are not laid all in one place. They are spread around, often in clusters. That way, even if some are destroyed, others may survive and grow.

Held by their mates, female damselflies deposit their eggs on the stalks of water plants.

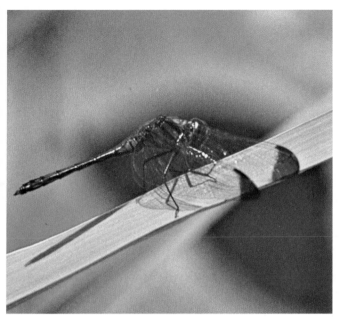 

Once mating and egg-laying are finished, the life cycle of the dragonfly and damselfly is completed, and the insects soon die. Most have lived for about a year, including the time that they spent as nymphs. During that year, an individual dragonfly or damselfly has probably eaten thousands of flies, mosquitoes, and other insects. In satisfying their own appetites, dragonflies and damselflies perform a valuable service for humans by keeping down the numbers of unwanted insects.

The next time you are near a pond in the summertime, watch for a bright flash of wings and a gleam of brilliant color at the water's edge. You may be rewarded by the sight of one of the most fascinating members of the insect world.

GLOSSARY

antennae (an-TEN-ee) — sense organs on the head of an insect, used for smelling and touching. The singular form of the word is *antenna*.

cerci (SUR-see) — claspers on the abdomen of a male dragonfly or damselfly used to grasp a female during mating

compound eyes — insect eyes made up of many tiny lenses

facet (FAS-uht) — one of the tiny six-sided lenses in an insect's compound eye

gills — breathing organs that extract dissolved oxygen from water. In their nymphal stage, dragonflies and damselflies breathe through gills.

iridescent (ir-ih-DES-unt) — having rainbow-like colors

labium (LAY-bee-um) — the lower lip of an insect. A dragonfly or damselfly nymph has a special hinged labium used to catch prey.

mandibles (MAN-dih-buhls) — jaws used for biting and chewing food

metamorphosis (met-uh-MOR-fuh-sis) — the process of development that produces most adult insects. Dragonflies and damselflies go through a three-stage development known as *incomplete metamorphosis*; the three stages are egg, nymph, and adult. Another process of development called *complete metamorphosis* has four stages: egg, larva, pupa, and adult.

molting—shedding an old skin to make way for a new one

nymph (NIMF)—the immature form of a dragonfly or damselfly; the second stage of incomplete metamorphosis

ocelli (oh-SEL-ee)—simple eyes of an insect, capable of telling the difference between dark and light

ovipositor (oh-vee-POS-ih-tur)—a tube at the end of a female insect's abdomen used to lay eggs

predator—an animal that hunts and kills other animals

spiracles (SPEAR-uh-kuhls)—breathing holes located on the sides of an insect's body

thorax—the middle section of an insect's body, to which the legs and wings are attached

wing pads—structures on a nymph's body that will develop into the wings of the adult insect

INDEX